First World War
and Army of Occupation
War Diary
France, Belgium and Germany

4 DIVISION
10 Infantry Brigade
Duke of Cambridge's Own (Middlesex Regiment)
3/10th (T.F.) Battalion
16 June 1917 - 22 February 1918

WO95/1482/2

The Naval & Military Press Ltd
www.nmarchive.com
Published in association with The National Archives

Published by

The Naval & Military Press Ltd

Unit 10 Ridgewood Industrial Park,

Uckfield, East Sussex,

TN22 5QE England

Tel: +44 (0) 1825 749494

www.naval-military-press.com

www.nmarchive.com

This diary has been reprinted in facsimile from the original. Any imperfections are inevitably reproduced and the quality may fall short of modern type and cartographic standards.

© Crown Copyright
Images reproduced by permission of The National Archives, London, England, 2015.

Contents

Document type	Place/Title	Date From	Date To
Heading	4th Division 10th Infantry Bde 3/10th Middlesex Reg Jun To December 1917		
Miscellaneous	D.A.G. 3rd Echelon	01/07/1917	01/07/1917
War Diary		16/06/1917	28/06/1917
Heading	War Diary of 3/10 Middlesex Regiment From 1st July 1917 To 31st July 1917 (Volume 2)		
War Diary	Middlesex Camp Blangy St Laurent Near Arras	12/07/1917	31/07/1917
War Diary	Blangy	01/08/1917	19/08/1917
War Diary	Stirling Camp	20/08/1917	22/08/1917
War Diary	In Line	26/08/1917	31/08/1917
Map	Map		
War Diary	In The Line	01/09/1917	06/09/1917
War Diary	Bellacourt	06/09/1917	29/09/1917
War Diary	Leipsig Camp	01/10/1917	02/10/1917
War Diary	Belgium Sheet 28 N.W. B.2.3.b.8.6	03/10/1918	04/10/1918
War Diary	Langemarck 1/10000 V.28.d.2.10	04/10/1917	14/10/1917
Miscellaneous	Report On Operations	05/10/1917	05/10/1917
War Diary	France Sheet 51b 1/40000	18/10/1917	29/10/1917
War Diary	Brown Line N.10.d.5.5	01/11/1917	01/11/1917
War Diary	Front Line	09/11/1917	09/11/1917
War Diary	Les Fosses	13/11/1917	13/11/1917
War Diary	Arras	18/11/1917	18/11/1917
War Diary	Les Fosses	25/11/1917	28/11/1917
War Diary	Front Line	29/11/1917	29/11/1917
War Diary	Arras	02/12/1917	02/12/1917
War Diary	Front Line	02/12/1917	02/12/1917
War Diary	Arras	04/12/1917	04/12/1917
War Diary	Front Line	10/12/1917	12/12/1917
War Diary	Brown Line	14/12/1917	16/12/1917
War Diary	Front Line	18/12/1917	22/12/1917
War Diary	Reserve Line	22/12/1917	26/12/1917
War Diary	Arras	28/12/1917	30/12/1917
Map	Map		
Heading	4th Division 10 Brigade 3/10 Middlesex Dis Feb 1918 Jan 1918-1918 Feb		
War Diary	Bois Des Beoufs	01/01/1918	01/01/1918
War Diary	Front Line	03/01/1918	07/01/1918
War Diary	Brown Line	11/01/1918	11/01/1918
War Diary	Front Line	12/01/1918	15/01/1918
War Diary	Support Line	16/01/1918	19/01/1918
War Diary	Arras	20/01/1918	22/01/1918
War Diary	Bois Des Boeufs	23/01/1918	27/01/1918
War Diary	Front Line	28/01/1918	31/01/1918
War Diary	Brown Line	01/02/1918	06/02/1918
War Diary	Schramm Barracks	06/02/1918	08/02/1918
War Diary	Agnes Les Duisans	08/02/1918	22/02/1918

4th Division
10th Infantry Bde
3/10th Middlesex Reg.

JUN ~~July~~ to December
1917
—
Feb 1918

D.A.G. S.A.
~~2nd Echelon~~ G.D.W.

Herewith War Diary
No 1 of this Regiment

T Platt
+ Lieut Col.
Cmdg. 3/10th Bn. Middlesex Regt.

1-7-17
B.E.F.   Attached to
9th Divn from 6.6.17

Transferred to 10 Bn 20.7.17

WAR DIARY
INTELLIGENCE SUMMARY

Army Form C.

3/10 Third/Mdsex

Place	Date	Hour	Summary of Events and Information	Remarks and references to Appendices

On the 31/5/17 9th 3/10 Middlesex Regt left CANTERBURY for SOUTHAMPTON. The Strength of the Regt on leaving was 33 Officers and 972 N.C.Os & men. The Regt entrained at SOUTHAMPTON on the 1/6/17 9th Battalion embarked (at HAVRE DECKS) about 11pm on the 1/6/17. 9th Battalion arriving at HAVRE Rest Camp at night & entraining again at 6am on 2/6/17, detrained at 4am on 3/6/17 & marched to LE PARCQ where we were (billetted) from 3rd to 6th.

On the 6th the Battalion proceeded by train from HESDIN & DUISANS and went into huttments at DUISANS (Y huttments) being attached to the South African Brigade of the 9th Division XVII Corps III Army. We remained in Y huttments from 6th to 16th.

On 16/6/17 the Battalion proceeded to BLANGY & encamped in the huttments of the German 1st Line. The Battalion were then split up for wiring & digging 6 days & night, along the Corps line of communication & support huttments over a front extending roughly from the POINT DU JOUR to MONCHY. This work was carried on until the termination of the R.E. Crew this during this work (is from 16th to 28th) give over two (2) Officers slightly wounded in hospital. Three other slightly wounded and (One) Officer Reymondally remained at Duty.

On the 27th Two companies were went into front line trenches for instruction. A.C.M. on night of 26/27 & B.C.M. on night of 27/28 on the front approximately from FAMPOUX to MONCHY.

16/6/17 to 28/6/17

No 2

3 appendices
a prisoner
July 20"

Confidential
War Diary
of
Middlesex Regiment

3/10 from 1st July 1917 to 31st July 1917.

(Volume 2)

3/10 Middlesex Regt

July 1917

WAR DIARY or INTELLIGENCE SUMMARY

Army Form C. 2118.

BLANGY CAMP,
near ARRAS.

Place	Date	Hour	Summary of Events and Information	Remarks and references to Appendices
MIDDLESEX CAMP BLANGY-ST LAURENT near ARRAS			3/10 Middlesex Regt 10th Bgde 4th Division. As stated in the diary for June, the Battalion arrived at BLANGY on the 17th & a camp was formed in the old "No-Man's-Land" between the original British & German front lines. Two companies of the Battalion were attached for training to the 4th Division & two to the 17th Division, & the XIII Corps 3rd Army line I wire & two permanent dug outs were constructed for the accommodation of the Battalion (2 Bn H.Q. & the forming a depot camp called Middlesex camp. On the 9/10 & 10/11th the two companies attached to the 4th Division returned to camp having on that spent part of their period of instruction in the first line holding a company on their own strength. (They were then employed in digging wider B.B. Sign also of the Corps — Casualties during this time being 5 other ranks killed by shell fire. The remaining two companies which had been attached respectively to the 50th and 51st Brigades of the 17th Division. The general front line on which the Battalion has been employed extends approximately from south of GAVRELLE through ROEUX & the hollows road work east of MONCHY-LE-PREUX. C Coy W & a Coy front from the 21st to 23rd & Bn returned to depot camp. D Coy were with the Bn on the Bn front on 27/28 & came out on the 29/31st inclusive from 23rd July to 3/10 Middlesex Regt ceased to be attached to the Division & ceased taking for the 4th Division. Total Casualties during the month were 1 officer killed (Lt W.E. Worthley) 3rd Middlesex Regt) and 3 other ranks, 5 officers wounded & 6 other ranks killed, 4 Officers wounded & 22 other ranks & 12 Other ranks	Refer Sheet 51SNW from H6c to 1314 H.A. Wm. Next 3/10 Middlesex Regt
	1/7/17 21st to 31st July			

Army Form C. 2118.

WAR DIARY 3/10
or
INTELLIGENCE SUMMARY
3/10 MIDDLESEX REGT.
(Erase heading not required.)

Ref: Map 57B/NW
      1/20000 Scale
Vol 3
August 1917.

Place	Date	Hour	Summary of Events and Information	Remarks and references to Appendices
Explanatory information			The Regt. now takes its place as one of the units of the Xth Brigade (Brig Genl A.G. Pritchard) in the 4th Division. The other Battalions of the Brigade being the 1st Warwicks, the 2nd Dragons, and the Honourable Artillery Battalion. The present front held by the Brigade is shewn on the attached sketch. The distribution of Battalions is in depth, dispositions being as follows: One Battalion in front line (supported & relieved by) – One Battalion in Brigade Support at H.23 a & c. – and two Battalions in Brigade Reserve. Brigade Support also finds one (or two) Companies to strengthen the local reserve. BLANGY. The Battalion in Bgde Support also finds one (or two) Companies to strengthen the line of the Battalion in the line.	Sketch attached
BLANGY	Warren		The Middlesex Regt relieved the nothing unusual to report.	4am
	1/8/17			
	7/8/17	9.30 p.m.	The Middlesex Regt moved from BLANGY to H.23 a & c. As Brigade Support, and two Companies were sent to Crump Trench (see sketch) under the orders of the Battalion in the line.	9.30pm
	8th		nothing unusual to report	
	9th			
	10th			
	11th			
	11/7/12		The Battalion moved up from Bgde Support & took over the front line from the 1st Warwicks. The front line consists principally of a chain of posts which are now being connected up to form a continuous trench. The German main line is in BARROT & CYPRUS in front of HAUSA and KUYLUSH trenches and are to be shell holes by night within about 60 yds of our posts. DELBAR WOOD is hit. Kuylush trench & the weakest parts of the front line are the flanks these are gradually being strengthened & more wire put up.	4am
	12th			
	13th		nothing to record	4pm

WAR DIARY
or
INTELLIGENCE SUMMARY

Army Form C. 2118.

5/10 Middlesex Regt for August 1917. (continued)

Place	Date	Hour	Summary of Events and Information	Remarks and references to Appendices
	14/8/17	5 am	2nd Lieut Major O'Neill and 3 other ranks went out from No 1 Post to reconnoitre the German posts on the canal about I.20.d 20.85. (See map and sketch) The post was occupied by two men only and both these men had stood down and were going to sleep in a shelter beside a shell hole. Our party crept up & surprised them; both were wounded & taken prisoner & brought back across the open to No 2 Post. The information given by these prisoners is contained in the Intelligence Summary attached.) JM.	Report of Patrol & Summary attached.
	14/8/17	10 PM	On the night of about 14th/15th an enemy patrol approached our wiring party between B and C Post. The wiring party, withdrawn to Sergt Kilvin, who was in charge, took up a firing position. He was joined shortly afterwards by 2/Lt Kirby who took command. This party (12th up) waited to [?] the enemy party. They heard voices & sounds of movement of challenging position to must the enemy party. 2 Lt Kirby then ordered fire to be opened. Cries & groans were heard but no call was aware. It Kirby has been hit, afterwards there was silence. The enemy having retired without showing a fight; in the morning a trench was made but no bodies were found. Sergt Buxton was also out with this party and did good work. Her /	
	15/8/17 18/8/17 17/8/17		Company relief carried out without incident. Enemy artillery & trench mortars fairly active throughout the day. Our artillery bombarded Kiel Flat in which is our No 1 Post. During the garrison not Lt. Stoneman were seen running in the open close to our post to escape our shells. An officer with a Lewis gun was enabled to assume to catch them in the open but he arrived too late, & they were able to get away. There has been telephonic communication between posts this was held up with her happened, after.	
	17/8/17 18/8/17 18/8/17		Enemy artillery slightly more active during the day. at night artillery activity increased over Ridge Post at I.30.a.10.8. — Enemy artillery shelling our front lines, Support & Reserve trenches, particularly in retaliation. Battalion relief carried out without incident. Regt moved back to STIRLING CAMP on relief. Entrainment at H.13.d. J C Nelson Major	

3/10th MIDDLESEX REGT. WAR DIARY   STIRLING CAMP Army Form C. 2118.
INTELLIGENCE SUMMARY   N² ARRAS.

Place	Date	Hour	Summary of Events and Information	Remarks and references to Appendices
STIRLING CAMP.	26/8/17 to 25/8/17	—	Training was carried out.	W.R.
"	25/8/17		The G.O.C. 45th Div. attended at STIRLING CAMP & presented Sgt. McKenzie with the Military Medal for services as reported.	W.R.
"	26/8/17		The 3/10th Bn MIDDLESEX Regt. relieved the HOUSEHOLD BATTALION in the line immediately N of the river SCARPE. The relief took place without incident.	W.R.
Line.	27/8/17		Major H. de B. O'Neill has been awarded the Military Cross for services reported.	W.R.
	28/8/17		A German was killed whilst in kent Post just N of the river SCARPE.	W.R.
	29/31 8/17		Battalion still in the line - nothing unusual to report. Total casualties during the month were 3 killed & 7 wounded (all privates)	W.R. W.R.

M Paulby H/Col
C.C. 3/10 Middx Regt

WAR DIARY
or
INTELLIGENCE SUMMARY
(Erase heading not required.)

Army Form C. 2118.

SKETCH OF FRONT HELD BY 10th BRIGADE
Aug 1917

Scale 1/10,000
(PLOUVAIN SECTOR)
3 hour R

Instructions regarding War Diaries and Intelligence Summaries are contained in F. S. Regs., Part II. and the Staff Manual respectively. Title Pages will be prepared in manuscript.

Place	Date	Hour	Summary of Events and Information	Remarks and references to Appendices

Note:
X. X german right patrol (general)
Y. Y german main patrol
SS german class support
Z. Z german path in shellholes

Own Regt numbered 1,2,3 etc ABC etc
═══ Route of Patrol

Labels on map: NAUSA WOOD, DELBAR WOOD, JUNCTION POSTS, PELVES, CEYLON, COLOMBO, RUINS OF ROEUX, SUPPORT LINE, CORUNNA SWITCH, GAP, CUSP, ROEUX WOOD, CRETE, CRUMP, Reserve companies, X BRIGADE BOUNDARY, XI BRIGADE BOUNDARY, SCARPE, SCARPE CANAL, Railway, Swamp, B.H.Q.

NORTH →

3/10th Bn. Middlesex Regt. **WAR DIARY** or **INTELLIGENCE SUMMARY**

Army Form C. 2118.

Sept 1917

Area near Arras and PROVEN
19th Bde., 4th Div., 17th Corps.

Vol 4

Place	Date	Hour	Summary of Events and Information	Remarks and references to Appendices
In the line.	1/9/17	—	News arrived that Major O'Neill was visited by the General, at the Officer's Rest Hospital, Watou, and awarded the M.C., on August 26th. Major A. E. Maitland reported to the Battalion on Aug. 29th & took over as 2nd in Command in succession to Major O'Neill (sick).	W.R.
	3/4/9/17		The Battalion was relieved by the HOUSEHOLD BATTALION and returned to STIRLING CASTLE. During the four we had two men wounded.	W.R.
	4/5/6/9/17		Continued training at STIRLING CAMP.	W.R.
BELLACOURT.	6/9/17		The Battalion marched to new Quarters at BELLACOURT for Training.	W.R.
	19th 20th/9/17		The Battalion entrained at SAULTY d'Abret and journeyed to PROVEN, to continue Training.	W.R.
	29/9/17		The Battalion entrained at PROVEN and journeyed to ELVERDINGHE to take part in operations. On the same night at 11.45 P.M. a bomb dropped on the Camp lines by a German Aeroplane, caused the following casualties. A Coy. Killed 6 P.Os. wounded 1 Sgt., 1 L/Sgt. & 28 P.tes. B. Coy. Killed 1 P.te. (drummer). Wounded 1 L/cpl & 7 men. also 1 L/cpl shellshock. C. Coy. 1 P.te wounded. D. Coy. 1 L/cpl wounded. In addition 2 Sgts & 4 P.tes of A Coy Wheners also wounded remain on duty. Total Killed 7. Wounded 42. 2/Lt. T.L.A. Bailey-Churchill Bn unit, attached 4th Div. Signal Coy was wounded by shell on the 30th. Total Casualties for month 7 Killed, 44 wounded.	W.R.

Place	Date	Hour	Summary of Events and Information	Remarks and references to Appendices
LEIPZIG CAMP BELGIUM SHEET 28 C.3/c N.W. B2 & B6 A-C-M	1 & 2 Oct 17		Nothing to report. On the night of the 3/4 Oct the Battalion left camp to take part in the attack NE of LANGEMARCK and moved to their new HQ at AUBONETE & was detailed to form the attacking Battalion. The Battalion was in support to 2nd Seaforths who were the attacking Battalion. The 2nd formed Boys Bn to command the rear of the 6th & 2nd Seaforths detailed as Boys Bn in the 5/10/17. 2 Platoons of B Coy being detailed as left flank guards to keep in touch with the 10th Brigade. The Battalion was made to a Battalion front & the 105 Brigade together was roughly 1,750 that their entrance BRUEMBEEK/10,000 v23 0 5hc. I was 1,000 yds north of EAGLE TRENCH the 11 Brigade starting front. The B/5 Brigade on our left. The Battalion was to cross over night & attack with assault at 6 am (Zero hour) on the 4/10/17 and without support having passed the two leading Companies Bn C moved forward to EAGLE TRENCH followed by D & B. Bn HQ started to move forward to EAGLE TRENCH & had about 1 am not gone more than 300 yds before the C.O. was touched by damn & sent to death & felt.... before the Battalion... offered from a stretch. Bn HQ could no longer to forward until BrigHeist... after the C.O. had moved forward owing to the intense Barrage. The B.M. reconnected from the north.... that BnHQ moved to EAGLE TRENCH recoiled from the attack had return from KANGAROO TRENCH had had owing to our Barrage being unmet	1917A. 1917A.
LANGEMARK 1/10,000 V23 D2.10	3/4			

3/10th Battalion Regt **WAR DIARY** area of ELVERDINGHE
Oct 1917 or
INTELLIGENCE SUMMARY 10th Bn. 4th Division
(Erase heading not required.)

Place	Date	Hour	Summary of Events and Information	Remarks and references to Appendices
LANGEMARK 1/10 ROO U28 J 2 10	3/10/17		OC Seaforths informed C.O. 3/10th Regt. that the whole of his Battalion had been attacked in the attack. The enemy kept an intense Barrage on EAGLE TRENCH 4 & 5 Oct. & it was almost impossible to move, a lot of shelter cases were pulled here coming down with our bearers. At about 2.30 p.m. the 4/5 Bn. C.O. required reinforcements as messages were being continually received from the 6 Company that their left flank was all cut, the left having failed to come into line. He, Lt/Royal Warwicks arrived at about 4 p.m. on the 4/10/17 & filled up the gap in the line with 2nd line of 115 Brigade & later pushed forward & got in touch with the remainder of the 2nd Seaforths & 13/10 Middx. Regt. The report attacked explains the remainder of the movement. We were relieved by the 13th Royal Warwicks on the night of 4th 5/6 & returned to the H.Q.s at BRIDGE CAMP	MMM
	5/6/5		Nothing to report.	MMM
	7/8/5			MMM
	9/10/17		On this date 1 Cpl. & 9 men were attached to 234th. G. Coy for carrying ammunition to front line, the Corporal & two O.R. were wounded. Also 3 Officers & 97 O.R. were attached to the 9th Field Coy. R.E. for carrying duck boards & carrying same to the front line, 50 R. were wounded.	MMM
	11/5 10/5 12/5 13/5 14/5		Nothing to report. On this date the Battalion moved from BRIDGE CAMP to POLL HILL CAMP near PROVEN Sheet 27 Home E.10 A 5.4. Nothing to report	MMM MOM MMM

M.W. Mann Lt

C O P Y.

From:- Lieut. Day,
       Commanding "D" Coy.,
To:-   O.C. DOVE.

Report on Operations 4-5/10/17.

Assembly. At 11.30 p.m. night 3-4th I took up position U.22.d.5.1. to U.28.b.7.5.

Advance. At ZERO Platoons moved forward to B2 in lines of 2 sections in file at 50 yards interval in the following order:-
  1st line 13 and 15,
  2nd line 14 and 16;
lines at 150 yards distance;
  The LEFT, moving along the LANGEMARK-SCHREIBOOM Road to direct.

Directing Flank. With my C.H.Q. I moved along this road to the taped line in B2. Here I found that Platoon Cdrs of 15 and 16 were casualties and that 13 and 14 had not reached the line. "A" Coy was close in my rear so without delay I rallied the Coy and moved forward to B1. Here I reorganised and again pushed forward to EAGLE TRENCH.

Advance. I immediately reported to O.C. DOGGED who ordered me to reinforce "C" Coy of that Battn. on the RIGHT of his Battn. I again reorganised and pushed forward to BEEK St. where I reported to Capt. LEWIS of this Battn. DOGGED line was about 150 yards/moving forward. By this time stragglers from 13 Platoon and the Lewis Gun Section of 14 Platoon had reached me and I was ordered to take the RIGHT FLANK forward.
  I did so suffering heavily from M.G. fire from ½ left front and then pushed on from shell hole to shell hole.

The new Line The line then stood firm, parties from the LEFT being sent forward to take concrete house at U.18.d.4.7. where an enemy M.G. was inflicting heavy casualties.
  Capt. LEWIS now (8.30 a.m.) ordered me to hold my position about U.18.d.5.4½. while he and Capt BALL reinforced the LEFT at U.18.d.2.5.
  No message came to me from forward or flank positions so with my batman, Pte HARDIMANN, I went out to reconnoitre the position.

The Position. At 9.30 a.m. our position was roughly as follows:-
The house at U.18.d.2.5. was ours and a party of DOGGED were consolidating there with "B" and "C" Coys. of this Battalion in rear. A thin line of DOGGED was holding shell holes about 80 yards down the forward slope of 19 METRE HILL, and 2/Lieut GOOCH with about 12 men were holding shell holes at U.18.d.7½.4.
  The M.G. fire was so deadly that beyond this I could obtain no further information so I returned and consolidated my position sending a small party under C.S.M. HEATHER out 50 yards to the right.
  At this time I had with me 14 and 16 Lewis Guns with a few men of each team together with my signallers under L/Cpl Porter who was doing good work and two runners. Other men in outlying shell holes tried to rally round me but were cut down by M.G. fire so I ordered remainder to consolidate their shell holes and dig through to me.

Reports. At 10-15 a.m. I sent a runner, Pte CUTLER, with a message to O.C. DOVE stating roughly my position, but he was hit emerging from shell hole, so I decided to wait until the M.G. fire had subsided.
  At 12 noon I sent for another runner, Pte GOTTS, in the

next

next shell hole to take a message to O.C. DOVE but he was hit coming to me.

We carried on with consolidation until about 2-45 p.m. when M.G. fire became intense. I soon observed parties of men from forward positions commence to withdraw and 2/Lieut. Kirby joined me from the LEFT.

Counter Attack.

The enemy now appeared in strong lines advancing from the FRONT and RIGHT and made unsuccessful attempts to break through on the LEFT. He came forward under cover of terrific M.G. fire and several of my men were hit whilst firing. Of these my batman, Pte HARDIMANN, though shot through the head assisted the Lewis Gun team by filling the magazines.

The Lewis Gun Team under Cpl. AMES and Pte. RATHBONE worked continuously and the former knocked out the crew of an enemy M.G. which came up to U.18.d.7.4½.

2/Lieut. KIRBY and C.S.M. HEATHER also kept up continuous rifle fire.

The enemy pushed forward to within about 80 yards of our position from the RIGHT by rushes and <u>I destroyed my maps and records</u>.

Our artillery barrage broke up the attack on the LEFT and FRONT, but on the RIGHT, he pressed on until supports of the HANTS drove him back.

We were now reduced to 55 rounds of ammunition despite men having gone out and taken ammunition from casualties.

During the counter-attack I saw an officer on my left, with a group of DOGGED and DOVE doing splendid work though twice wounded. I afterwards found him to be 2/Lieut. BEST (?) DURHAM FIELD COY., R.E.

Reports.

At 4 p.m. I sent another runner, Pte. LESTER, with a message to O.C. DOVE stating position and asking for ammunition.

At 5 p.m. the enemy appeared to assemble for a second counter-attack but was quickly dispersed by our artillery barrage.

At 6 p.m. Pte. LESTER had not returned so I sent Pte. COOK with a similar message.

At about 7 p.m. an Officer of the R.B. said he had supports coming up in rear of men and would send me ammunition. This I did not receive and at 9 p.m., neither of the two runners having returned, I sent down 2/Lt. KIRBY to explain the seriousness of my position without ammunition to O.C. DOVE.

At 10 p.m. 2/Lieut. MONTIETH of DOGGED reported being in a similar position re ammunition. At 10-30 p.m.

At 10-30 p.m., having no news of previous runners, I sent down L/Cpl. PORTER with another man asking O.C. DOVE for ammunition and reinforcements, my strength now being down to about 25 O.R.

Reinforcements.

At 3.15 a.m. 5th L/Cpl Porter returned with 2/Lieut MAY and his (13) Platoon with ammunition. He later reinforced my right and got in touch with the HANTS.

The remainder of the day and night of the 5th were comparatively quiet and we tended the wounded lying out as much as possible giving them what little water we had.

In the meantime 2/Lieut. COOCH with his men-Several of whom were wounded - had continued to hold their position with utmost gallantry. All other Officers of this Battalion had been killed or wounded.

Relief.

At 12.15 a.m. 6th., I was relieved by a company of the

R. WARWICKS.

I called for volunteers to carry down tose wounded who had been lying out for many hours unable to walk down themselves.

We succeeded in bringing down:-

WOUNDED

2/Lieut. BEST(?) DURHAM FIELD COY. R.E.

Pte GOTTS, "D" Coy. DOVE,
and a full corporal of DOGGED.

I left instructions with the R. WARWICKS who promised to clear the remainder of the wounded.

On the jouney home I was ably assisted by Sgt. HOPWOOD and L/Cpl. PORTER for the men were exhausted owing to conditions and inclement weather and also shell fire through which we had to return.

RECOMMEN-DATIONS.

I consider that special commendation and reward is due to the following:-

2/Lieut. GOOCH, "C" Coy. DOVE.
2/Lieut. KIRBY, "B" Coy. DOVE.
2/Lieut. BEST(?) DURHAM FIELD COY., R.E.

290046 C.S.M. Heather E.V.
L/12316 Sergt. Hopwood W.
290973 Corpl. Ames J.E.
G/34183 L/Cpl. Porter B.
292642 Pte Hardimann W.G.
293776 Pte Rathbone I.W.

(Signed) W. CONWAY DAY,
LIEUT.,
3/10th Battn. Middlesex Regiment.

Army Form C. 2118.

3/10 Bn Bn Rudolling Regt

WAR DIARY
or
INTELLIGENCE SUMMARY
(Erase heading not required.)

Arras Area.
Oct 1917   10th Bde. 4th Division.

Place	Date	Hour	Summary of Events and Information	Remarks and references to Appendices
France Sheet 51B 1/40000	18th		On the morning of the 18th the Battalion marched to HOUPOUTRE & entrained. It detrained at AUBIGNY & marched to Y Huts etc (near ETRUN) reaching there about 4pm. The Battalion remained here training until the 23rd when they marched to SCHRANN BARRACKS where they remained for the night. On the night 24/25 the Battalion took over the CAMBRAI ROAD SECTOR (between PICK AVENUE inc. & GORDON AVENUE inc.) from the E. SURREYS. During the tour of four days a certain amount of wiring was done but owing to a good deal of rain much work had to be done in the trenches, which had fallen in in a great many places. Patrols were sent out to reconnoitre the man's land & also to find out if certain shell holes in front of our No 3 Sap were occupied. The state of no man's land was found to be of our No 3 Sap were occupied. There being marshy & full of shell holes, no enemy was encountered. The shell holes in front of our No 3 were occupied & were heavily wired all Patrols returned safely. During the tour enemy activity was below normal. The night it front was held by "A" Coy, GORDON AVENUE to on the right flank & POMMEL ALLEY men left. B Coy held the left front sector from POMMEL ALLEY (right) to PICK AVENUE (left) inclusive. The Battalion was relieved on the night of the 28/29 by the 2nd Bedfords. Two Coys occupied SPADE RESERVE two Coys were at LES FOSSES FARM. There were 600 supply my a garrison of 1 Off 9 34 O.R. each, at B & C Strong Points. Working a saving parties were supplied by 2 Coys from the support garrisons (LES FOSSES FARM, SPADE RESERVE & B & C Strong Points) following a list of casualties which occurred during the month.	M.D.N. M.D.N. M.D.N. M.D.N. M.D.N. M.D.N.
	23			
	24/25			
	28/29			

M.D.Manager Major

Army Form C. 2118.

3/10 Bn. Bradfords Regt.

WAR DIARY
or
INTELLIGENCE SUMMARY

Arras area

Oct 1917. 10th Bde. 4th Division.

Place	Date	Hour	Summary of Events and Information	Remarks and references to Appendices
			Officers (12)	
			Capt Lewis H.B. Killed	
			Ball L.A. Missing	
			Lieut Egerton H.T. Wounded	
			" Watson T.C. Missing	
			" 2nd Lieut Austin S.K. Wounded	
			2/Lt Dixon W.H. do	
			" Jones P.F. do	
			" Woodward H. do	
			" Kirby H.S.R. do & rejoined	
			" Smith R.E. Wounded	mm
			" Nathanson J.E. do	
			" Groves D.H. do	
			Warrant Officers	
			Wounded 1	
			Sergeants	
			Killed 2	
			Wounded 5	
			Missing 1	
			6/8/96	
			Missing 1	
			Corporals	
			Wounded 16	
			Missing 4	
			L/Corporals	
			Killed 1	
			Wounded 20	
			Missing 9	
			Men	
			Killed 14	
			Wounded 159	
			Missing 60	
			Total Casualties	MM Mann Lt Col
			12 Officers & 293 OR	

WAR DIARY or INTELLIGENCE SUMMARY

Army Form C. 2118.

3/10 Middlesex Regt.
Nov. 1917

Place	Date	Hour	Summary of Events and Information	Remarks and references to Appendices
[illegible]	1/11/17	—	[illegible handwritten entry regarding return march]	
[illegible]	9/11/17	—	The Battalion relieved the [illegible] in support trenches	Laythes
Les Fosses	13/11/17	—	The Battalion was relieved by the 2nd Seaforth and went into Brigade Reserve, moving to [illegible] and was employed on salvage work. [illegible] many huts etc were erected in the [illegible] Corps area. Nov 14/11/17.	Laythes
ARRAS	18/11/17	—	On Sunday Nov 18th 1917 the Battalion was relieved by the 1st Royal Warwicks Regt and became Brigade Reserve. On Saturday evening 24/11/17 the Battalion had orders to "stand to" and to prepare to move at short notice. Orders were not carried out but a standfast order was received on Sunday 25/11/17. Nov 15-16-17 Battalion were quartered in huts at Arras. We carried on usual duty.	Copse
Les Fosses	25/11/17		The Battalion relieved the Honourable Battalion in the [illegible] and became support [illegible] Northampton. [illegible] were provided and its work in [illegible] of C.F.O.E. RESERVE, [illegible] by various [illegible] employers, was carried out [illegible]	

31/11/17 [signature] Lt Col

WAR DIARY

Army Form C. 2118.

3/10th Battn. 10th Brigade
Middlesex Regt. 4th Division
Front Line Report Arras

Place	Date	Hour	Summary of Events and Information	Remarks and references to Appendices
Les Fosses	3/11/17	—	An extended area was given to the Brigade Battalion and the extra was to be taken from the Rifle Brigade 11th hour working line to support. This took place.	Appx.
	3/11/17	—	On Thursday Nov 29th the battalion relieved the Seaforth Highlanders and became front line battalion. From 5 a.m. Nov 30th a period of quiet was experienced. Enemy artillery fire was fairly heavy and intense. On Saturday Dec 1st at 4 p.m. I remembered there was to be a sweep, & the thermals shells took place which lasted until 9:15 pm. Enemy gave up artillery, trench mortars and machine gun fire. Our artillery during this night did a considerable return information and reported the enemy fire, also we got in touch with my troops but nothing could be obtained. We were in front of our left-rest. On night of 2nd Novr. the battalion was relieved by 11th KRRC from 5 pm to 6.35 pm. Corps artillery bombardments was carried out. Enemy retaliation was heavy & front line. The Battalion on relief went into quarters in PRISON in ARRAS. Casualties during the week — 1 Officer killed	Appx.
				2 O.R. wounded
Arras	3/12/17		Casualties during the week 4 wounded O.R's	Signed Capt. & Adjutant 3/10th Middlesex

3/12/17 A.J. Gresham Capt. & Adjutant

WAR DIARY or INTELLIGENCE SUMMARY

Army Form C. 2118.

1/10 Battn
4th Division
Middlesex Regt
FRONTLINE ARRAS
Dec. 1917

Place	Date	Hour	Summary of Events and Information	Remarks and references to Appendices
FRONTLINE	2/12/17		The work done by the two patrols sent out at 4. A.M. area 2nd 1917 previously referred to under month of November was commenced by Major General Matheson commanding the Division, the Officers in charge were 2/Lt PERRY and 2/Lt Briggs respectively.	C/Jackson
ARRAS	4/12/17	—	The battalion reached billets at Le Prison and moved into billets at ST GUEDARD. The battalion deserved the first day out of the line was put to interior economy. Parking parades, kit and equipment inspections, unitarily routine and disciplines. Nothing of importance occurred. During the remainder of the stay in ST GUEDARD the battalion carried out training. The companies range practices, clean order physical training and a few practices with Lewis gun firing. On Wednesday Dec 5th the battalion carried on a Tactical exercise, but Divisional communications were implemented on the Divisional field firing area in a similar exercise based. A Tactical scheme, the battalion acting as advance guard to the Brigade was carried out on Dec 9th in BOISVILLE area	C/Jackson C/Jackson C/Jackson
FRONTLINE	10/12/14		The battalion relieved the 1st Hampshire Regt in the MONCHY sector on the 10/11/17 and took left subsector on the left brigade front. Relief was left front battalion and three casualties were caused during relief and shortly after night to assisting the enemy wire. A Patrol was sent out during the night of 10/11 Dec to ascertain if the enemy was holding and nothing definite was obtained, but several Germans were seen the enemy held and the wire was found to be in good condition.	C/Jackson

WAR DIARY
INTELLIGENCE SUMMARY

2/10 Batt. MONCHY LE PREUX
10th Brigade 4th Division
Front Line ARRAS
Dec. 1917

Place	Date	Hour	Summary of Events and Information	Remarks and references to Appendices
Front Line	12/12/17		Two patrols went out during the night. One under 2/Lt WYMAN to ascertain if ARRON Tr. was held. The trench was found to be destroyed, not held. The patrol was fired at from DEVIL Tr. A strong patrol of 6 men under 2/Lt. Philletin to obtain a prisoner, found enemy were very strong in front of DEVIL Tr. & LYS strongly held. They were fired at by M.G.s and had to withdraw. Two men were wounded.	
Brown line	14/15/12/17		The Battalion came out, to Reserve for 4 days. Employed on working parties.	
Front Line	18/12/17		The Battalion relieved the 1st Warwickshire Regt in the MONCHY sector, and became left front battalion on the left brigade front. Hostile barrage was encountered during relief. A patrol was sent out during the night and located enemy Machine Gun at J.33.C.20.38. 2/Lt. Wye Jowler in charge.	
" — "	19/12/17 22/12/17 6.22 p.m.		A heavy front reveren led another patrolling. The Battalion was relieved by the 1st Bn Warwickshire Regt and occupied the reserve trenches N of MONCHY for 4 days. During the relief about midday enemy artillery activities caused 4 casualties D.K.2.W.	
" — "	23/12/17		At 6.20pm the enemy put on the front line heavy artillery barrage (1 casualty wounded.)	

3/10 Middx Regt
Dec 1917.

WAR DIARY
or
INTELLIGENCE SUMMARY

10th Brigade
4th Division
Front Arras

Army Form C. 2118.

Place	Date	Hour	Summary of Events and Information	Remarks and references to Appendices
RESERVE LINE	26/12/17		The Battalion was relieved by the 2nd Bn Lancashire Fusiliers and proceeded to Arras for 10 days, where we received reinforcements 88 men	
Arras	28/12/17		The Battalion had a holiday, and held their Xmas dinner Xmas day	
"	30/12/17		The Battalion proceeded to the Bois-des-Boeufs.	

Bois. des-Boeufs.
31-12-1917

H. [signature]
Major
Commanding 3/10 Middlesex Regt

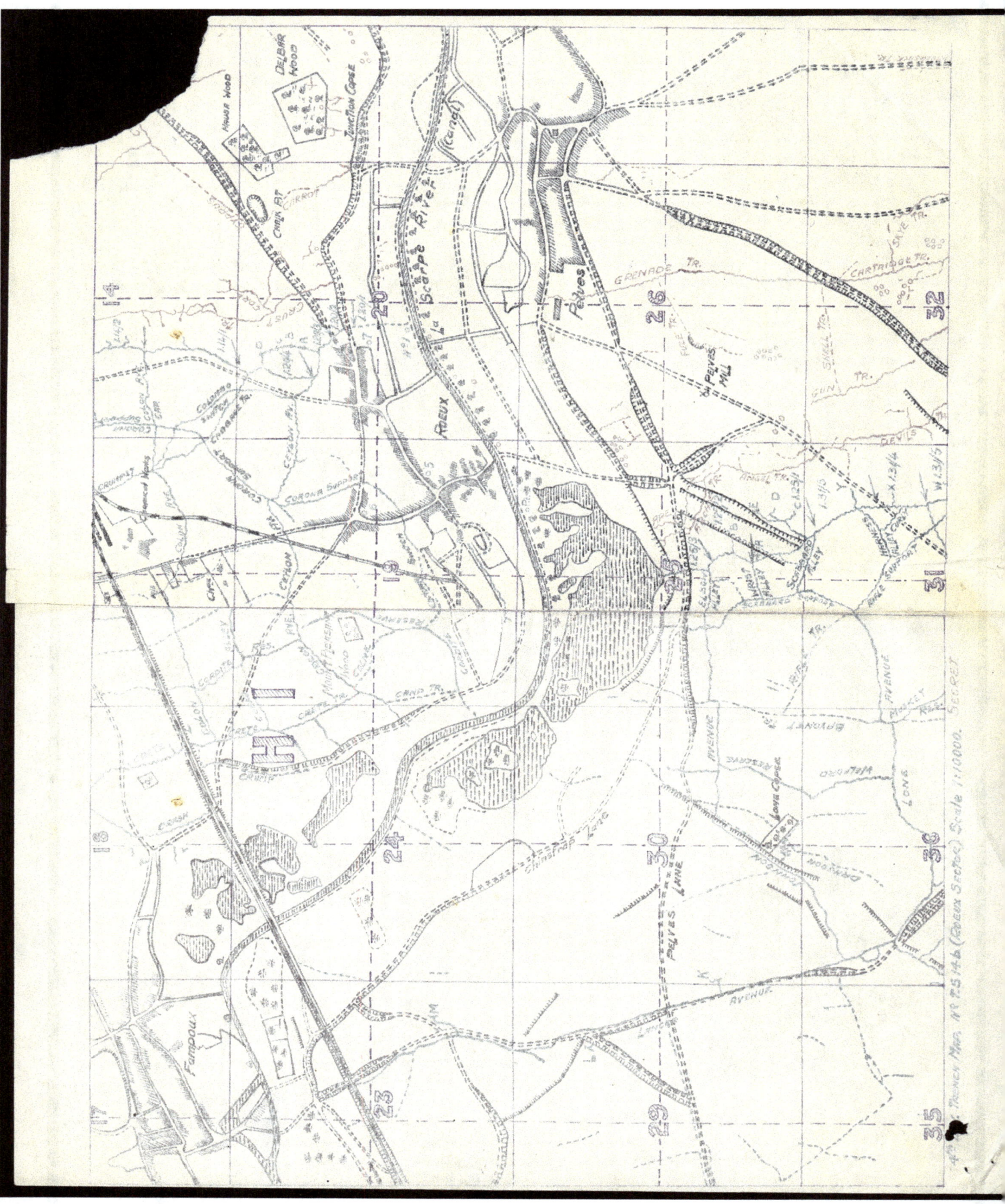

4th Division
10 BRIGADE
2/10 Middlesex
Dis. Feb. 1918

Jan 1918
1917 JUNE — 1918 FEB

DISBANDED

Army Form C. 2118.

2/10th Bn Middlesex Regt   4th Division
                            190th Brigade
                            Front Line Arras

WAR DIARY
or
INTELLIGENCE SUMMARY
(Erase heading not required.)

January 1918

Place	Date	Hour	Summary of Events and Information	Remarks and references to Appendices
Bois-des-Boeufs	1st		The Battalion were in reserve.	Wharry
Front Line	3rd		The Battalion relieved the 1/Bn Hampshire Regt in the Left Sub-Sector on the right Brigade.	Wharry
"	4th		A Patrol under 2/Lt Heighes was sent out to reconnoitre No Mans Land. No enemy were encountered.	Wharry
"	5th		A patrol under 2/Lt Dicks went out to reconnoitre & revisit enemy advanced posts.	Wharry
"	6th		A patrol under 2/Lt Hay went out to reconnoitre and observed an enemy working party who were fired on by Lewis Gun.	Wharry
"	7th		The Battalion were relieved by the 1st/8th Royal Warwickshire Regt and proceeded to the BROWN LINE, forming the 2nd + 3rd Line of support was put out in front of the front Line.	Wharry
Brown Line	11th		The Battalion relieved the 1st/8th Royal Warwickshire Regt in the Left Sub-sector right Brigade	Wharry
Front Line	12th		Battalion reconstructed wire in front of Saps.	
"	13th		Enemy attempted a raid on our Sap 7 but were vigorously repulsed by Lewis Gun, Rifle Fire & Rifle Grenades. We suffered no casualties.	
"	14th		Nothing of interest happened	
"	15th		A Strong Patrol under 2/Lt Cook went out to engage enemy patrols. None were encountered.	

Army Form C. 2118.

WAR DIARY
or
INTELLIGENCE SUMMARY.
(Erase heading not required.)

1/4th B. Warwick R^t 4 Warwick
January 1918 Bgde.

Instructions regarding War Diaries and Intelligence Summaries are contained in F. S. Regs., Part II. and the Staff Manual respectively. Title pages will be prepared in manuscript.

Place	Date	Hour	Summary of Events and Information	Remarks and references to Appendices
SUPPORT LINE	18		Reorganising Trenches	Hr Clerk
	19.		Relieved by 2nd R. Warwicks	H. Clerk
ARRAS	20.		The Battalion was in Brigade	H. Clerk
	21.		Reserve	H. Clerk
BOURDER B?	22. 23.		The Battalion went in Reserve	MMammn
	26.		The Battalion relieved the 1st Hants on the night 27/28. Left out sector of left sector	MMamm
	27.		Two patrols were sent out to inspect enemy wire & reconnoitre no mans	
FRONT LINE	28.		land. A party of about 17 men were seen approaching our wire & were dispersed by fire	MMamn
	29.		Three patrols went out to reconnoitre no mans land. No enemy met with. ARROW TRENCH found unoccupied.	MMamm
	30.		Two patrols sent out to patrol no mans land. No enemy encountered	MMamm
	31.		A patrol was sent out to patrol foreplace wire. No signs of the enemy	MMamm
BROWN LINE	1/2/18		Relieved by the 1st Warwicks. returned to BROWN LINE, arrived 1/2/18	MMamm

Casualties for the month

	Officers	D.O.W.	Sgts. Cpls. L/Cpls. Pts.	Total
Killed	NIL			3 — 4
Wounded	1		1 — 3	16 — 20

Total Casualties — 1 Officer
23 O.R.

N. Wright Major
1/4 Warwick R^t

3/10th Bn. Middx. Regt. WAR DIARY
or
INTELLIGENCE SUMMARY.

45th Division
10th Brigade

Army Form C. 2118.

February 1918.

(Erase heading not required.)

Place	Date	Hour	Summary of Events and Information	Remarks and references to Appendices
BROWN LINE	1/6 to 6/2		The Battalion occupied this line during the period Feb 1–6. Working parties were supplied for the front line system every night.	Mahaun
SCHRAMM BARRACKS	6–8		Relieved by Royal Scots, marched to Schramm Barracks, where we were billeted for two days.	Mahaun
	8/2		This day the Battalion marched out from B attacks at 17:30 a.m. to proceed to AGNES lès DUISANS, where the Battalion was to meet pending disbandment. Before leaving the Barracks the Battalion was drawn up forming three sides of a square, to be inspected & addressed by the Divisional General, Major Genl T.G. MATTHESON cmdg. 45 Division. Before the Battalion left the Division, the General spoke as follows:— Lt Col Collibes, Officers, Warrant Officers N.C.O.s & men of the 3/10 Middlesex Regiment, it is with very great regret that I address you this morning to bid you farewell. As you know orders have been issued for the B Battalion to be disbanded. The reasons are due to no fault of your own, but to the military policy of our Country & this has been explained to you in a letter of farewell from the C-in-C & our C-in-Chief. You have been in the Division since Aug 1917 & have well maintained your position in the 10th Infantry Brigade, a fact of which I am well... the Brigadier in whose Brigade... experience you had when you joined the Division compared with the 2 years experience of the B3 Battalion here in the Division will...	Mahaun

Army Form C. 2118.

3/10 Bn. Middx. Regt.   4th Division
                         105 Brigade
February 1918   Arras

WAR DIARY
or
INTELLIGENCE SUMMARY.
(Erase heading not required.)

Instructions regarding War Diaries and Intelligence Summaries are contained in F.S. Regs., Part II. and the Staff Manual respectively. Title pages will be prepared in manuscript.

Place	Date	Hour	Summary of Events and Information	Remarks and references to Appendices
SCHRAMM BARRACKS	8		So whenever out of many be the lot of each one that to be transferred it will be best made that is to remember that you have been in the Regt. which so gallantly fought in the Battle of Flanders Oct 1917. I also do you just many of having shed a great deal. I am sure that you will accept the above of the movement to act, & feel confident that you will show to whom great enemy in carrying out your duties in your new unit, as you have while under my command. Thank you for the loyal way in which you have worked together while under my command, you have close of honourably & done all good and I wish [illegible] future.	Mahon?
AGNES LES DUISANS	8-20		This Battalion arrived at AGNES LES DUISANS about mid-day & were billeted in the 4th Divisional Depot Camp. During the following Feb 8-20th parades were carried out during the mornings. Battalion sports were held on Feb 12th following is a list of events winners. (Feb 12th)	Mahon?

100x open (Std) 1) Pte Houghwood C. Coy.   High Jump
                (C) Bernard   1) Pte Winstock C. Coy.
                                            2) Sgt. Hockhart do

100x (Open) 1) Pte Richardson C.   do
      (SR.) 2) Sgt. Perkins A.   Long Jump
                                            1) Pte Bingham   D.
220x (original) 1) Pte Bermuda C.   2) Sgt. Rolfeld C.
     3/10 Mdx. 2) Sgt. Bent
                                            Boot Hill Race
Obstacle   1) Sgt. Douglas A.   1) Sgt. Ryan C.
Race.   Sgt. Machan   C.   2) Pte Collins C.

                                            Wheelbarrow Race
                                            1) Sgt Ryan } D. Coy
                                               Pte White }
                                            2) C.S.M. Hopwood }
                                               C.Q.M.S. Text. } B.

3/10th Bn. Middx. Regt. 115th Entrenching Battn.
February 12th 1918. Feb. 20th - 28th
1918. 1918. ARRAS.

WAR DIARY or **INTELLIGENCE SUMMARY.**
Army Form C.
(Erase heading not required.)

Place	Date	Hour	Summary of Events and Information	Remarks and references to Appendices
AGNES LES DUISANS	12th		Three legged Race. Sack Race. Football. Garside.	Unavoidable
			1) Pte Hammer. S. } A. 1) Pte Wilmore .. D.Co Sgt. Northcott. L/Cpl. Byrne	
			W. } 2) " Middleton. C. Sgt. Northcott Pte Woodward.	
			2) Cpl. Howell } B. actg field Cpl. Parkins. Pankhurst.	
			L/Cpl. Stoner }	
	20th		It was decided by the Authorities that the Battalion should not be broken up but made into an Entrenching Battn & so accordingly on this date we became the 115th Entrenching Battn. under the orders of G.E. 3rd Army & 17th Corps. Lt Col. B. H. Barkley. (K.S.L.I. att'd cmdg. 3/10 Middx) was appointed O.C. 3rd Army Group. Entrenching Bns. H.Q. ALBERT & Capt. Hardy – Lamont. (adjt 3/10 Middx) was appointed his Adjutant. Major H. Forst (Scottish Horse. att. 42nd Command 3/10 Middx) was appointed C.O. of the new Battn & Capt. Livingstone (H) Middx att. 3/10 Middx) as Lt adj & Q.M. At the time of the forming of the new Battn. the above three officers were on leave, & so Capt. J. H. Greenwood was temporarily appointed C.O. a Lt R. Hitcham his Adjutant. On the night of the 20/21. about 12 p.m. an order was received from XVII Corps that the Battn had to move to ARRAS the following day & that the move had to be complete by 12 mid-day. Orders were accordingly issued & the Battn marched out from AGNES LES DUISANS. the following morning at 9.30 am. punctually, the move was complete by 12 noon. C/o the Battn, when part of the ARRAS, had orders owing to obstructions to transport etc. to bivouac & other hands it proved itself backwards without any of the above, however in the course of a few days there were made good. On the 22nd the Battn commenced work inside the abbey of huge Saxton 30 (strong) the work consisted of wiring a trench dug on the following are the names of N.C.O's & men specially mentioned for good work in the line in January.	Unavoidable
	21.			
	22.			

L/Cpl.(un/Act.) PEARMAN } "A"   CSM. BURTON }
L/Cpl(L/Cpl) GIBSON } MARKEY } Coy   Pte SNOWDEN } "C" Coy   Casualties during the month.
                  MAY }   BUTTON.   Cpls.   Privates.
                                          NEWTON.   1   3
                                          RANDELL.

www.ingramcontent.com/pod-product-compliance
Lightning Source LLC
Chambersburg PA
CBHW081502160426
43193CB00014B/2570